REAL WORLD DATA

GRAPHING IMMIGRATION

Andrew Solway

www.heinemannlibrary.co.uk
Visit our website to find out more
information about Heinemann
Library books.

To order:
☎ Phone +44 (0) 1865 888066
📄 Fax +44 (0) 1865 314091
📖 Visit www.heinemannlibrary.co.uk

Heinemann Library is an imprint of Capstone Global Library
Limited, a company incorporated in England and Wales
having its registered office at 7 Pilgrim Street, London, EC4V
6LB – Registered company number: 6695582

"Heinemann" is a registered trademark of Pearson Education
Limited, under licence to Capstone Global Library Limited

Edited by Megan Cotugno and Diyan Leake
Designed by Victoria Bevan and Geoff Ward
Original illustrations © Capstone Global Library, LLC 2010
Illustrated by Geoff Ward
Picture research by Ruth Blair, Zooid Pictures Ltd
Originated by Chroma Graphics (Overseas) Ltd
Printed in China by Leo Paper Products Ltd

ISBN 978 0 431 03343 3 (hardback)
14 13 12 11 10
10 9 8 7 6 5 4 3 2 1

British Library Cataloguing in Publication Data
Solway, Andrew.
 Graphing immigration. -- (Real world data)
 304.8'0728-dc22
A full catalogue record for this book is available from the
British Library

Acknowledgements
The author and publishers are grateful to the following for
permission to reproduce copyright material: Alamy pp. **8**
(© North Wind Picture Archives), **12** (© Mark Eveleigh), **22**
(© Keith Dannemiller); Corbis pp. **6** (Sayre Berman), **20** (Jb
Russell/Sygma); Geophysical Fluid Dynamics Laboratory
p. **27** (National Ocean and Atmospheric Administration);
Getty Images pp. **14** (Olivier Laban-Mattei/AFP), **24** (Joe
Raedle); Rex Features p. **4** (Sipa Press); Roke p. **5** (Wikipedia
Commons); Shutterstock pp. **16** (© WizData, inc.), **25**
(© Laurence Gough), **26** (© Samuel Acosta).

Cover photograph of a march drawing attention to claims
of exploitation and discrimination of migrant workers,
Trafalgar Square, London on 7 May 2007, reproduced
with permission of Getty Images (Matt Cardy).

We would like to thank Dr Michael Reibel for his invaluable
help in the preparation of this book.

Every effort has been made to contact copyright holders
of any material reproduced in this book. Any omissions
will be rectified in subsequent printings if notice is given
to the publishers.

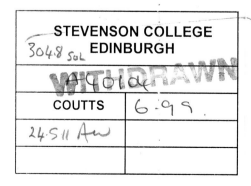

CONTENTS

Some words are printed in bold, **like this**. You can find out what they mean by looking in the glossary, on page 30.

Are there people in your class who come from another country? Perhaps you yourself moved from another country to the place where you live now. When people move to one country from another country, it is called immigration.

Worldwide, nearly 200 million people are **immigrants** to the country where they live. This sounds like a lot, but it is only about 3 percent of the total world **population**. About 97 percent of people stay all their lives in the country where they were born.

From poor countries to richer ones

People **migrate** for many different reasons. In general, people move from poorer countries to richer ones. About 20 percent of all immigrants are in the US, and around 19 percent are in Europe.

 Illegal immigrants from Senegal, Africa, arrive at Tenerife, Canary Islands.

Fear and suspicion

Many immigrants move to a new country looking for a better life. Some are forced to move because they do not feel safe in their old home. Most immigrants find homes and work when they move and settle down without too much difficulty. However, some immigrants are **exploited**. They find themselves working almost as slaves and living in very bad conditions.

Why do people migrate? What sort of reception do they get in their new country? How do they fit in? What is illegal immigration, or people-trafficking? And what will happen in the future? Will more people migrate, or fewer? You can find the answers in this book.

Amazing fact

If all the immigrants in the world had their own country, it would have a bigger population than any country except China, India, Brazil, Indonesia, and the US.

The world's migrants

Every country has some immigrants arriving and some **emigrants** leaving each year. Generally countries that are wealthier (blue on the map) have more immigrants than emigrants, while poorer countries (brown) have more emigrants than immigrants. Countries shown in green have roughly equal numbers of emigrants and immigrants.

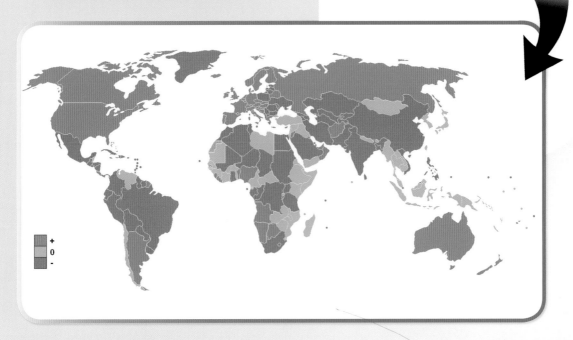

+
0
-

What connects the **ambassador** Madam Fu Ying, the scientist Marie Curie, and a group of children getting off a bus in Damascus, Syria? The answer is that they are all immigrants.

These people moved country for very different reasons. Madam Fu Ying moved from China to Britain as part of her job. Marie Curie moved from Poland to France because she wanted to study at the Sorbonne (the University of Paris). The children moved from Iraq to Syria because their parents decided that living in Iraq had become too dangerous. These examples show that there are many different kinds of immigrants.

Famous immigrants from the past

Marie Curie is only one of many famous immigrants from the past. The scientist Albert Einstein, the inventor Alexander Graham Bell, and the writer Isaac Asimov all migrated to the US. Famous immigrants to the UK include the composer George Frideric Handel, the artist Hans Holbein, and the poet T.S. Eliot.

 Akon is a famous hip-hop singer and songwriter. He was brought up in Senegal, but he emigrated to the US when he was 15.

Who are the immigrants?

We have already seen that immigrants usually move from poorer countries to richer ones. However, this does not mean that all immigrants are poor. It is expensive to travel to a new country, and once there people need money to help them survive. Usually, the poorest people cannot afford to migrate.

Many immigrants are also better educated than average. Some are not as well educated. One of the main reasons that immigrants move to developed countries is to improve their education.

Every immigrant country has a particular mix of nationalities. This mix depends on where it is located in the world and the links it has with other countries. In the US, for instance, Mexicans are the biggest immigrant group at present, followed by people from other Latin American countries and the Caribbean. In the U.K. the largest immigrant group is not so clear-cut. There are large numbers of immigrants from India, Pakistan, Poland, the Irish Republic, and many other countries. Germany has many immigrants from Turkey, Greece, Italy, and Poland, while in France many immigrants come from northern Africa, Turkey, and Spain.

Where do immigrants come from?

This pie chart shows that 31% of US immigrants (nearly a third) come from Mexico. Smaller numbers come from other Latin American countries and Asia.

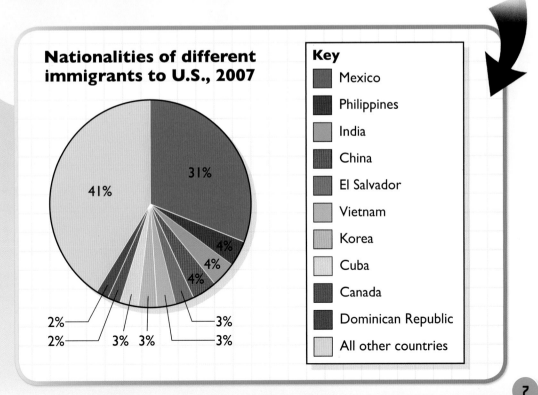

Nationalities of different immigrants to U.S., 2007

41%
31%
4%
4%
4%
2%
2%
3%
3%
3%
3%

Key
- Mexico
- Philippines
- India
- China
- El Salvador
- Vietnam
- Korea
- Cuba
- Canada
- Dominican Republic
- All other countries

Reasons for moving

There are many reasons why people might want to move from one country to another. Most people move either because they want to go to another country, or because they are driven out of their own country.

Often immigrants are young people with families. They move because they want to improve life for themselves, and especially for their children. They choose to go to a richer country than their own, where they believe living conditions will be better and they can earn more money.

There can be many reasons for choosing to move to one country rather than another. Immigrants may choose a place where people speak the same language as they do. West Africans, for example, often **emigrate** to France. This is because French is spoken in many west African countries. Other immigrants may choose to go to a country where they already know people. Often, if one person moves to a new country and settles, other people from the same area will follow. Some immigrants choose a country because it is encouraging immigrants to go there. In the 1950s and 1960s, the Australian government encouraged Europeans to move there, and even paid some of their moving costs. From 2001 to 2008, the Spanish government encouraged immigrants because they needed workers, especially in the building industry.

This drawing shows the fort at Jamestown, Virginia, in 1622. Jamestown was the place where the first English immigrants to the American colonies arrived in 1607.

An immigrant country

Historically, the population of the US is made up almost entirely of immigrants. The first European immigrants arrived in the early 1500s, and new groups of immigrants have continued to arrive ever since. These include the earliest Spanish settlers, the English and Germans who built **Jamestown**, slaves from west Africa, Irish people fleeing from **famine** (see page 10), Scandinavians escaping from wars and failed crops, and people from many other nations.

Immigrants to Australia

This line graph shows the numbers of immigrants to Australia from the UK, New Zealand, China, and India. Since 1991, the numbers of immigrants from all four countries have risen. From 1994 to 2000, the numbers coming from New Zealand rose quickly, but then fell sharply from 2001 to 2003.

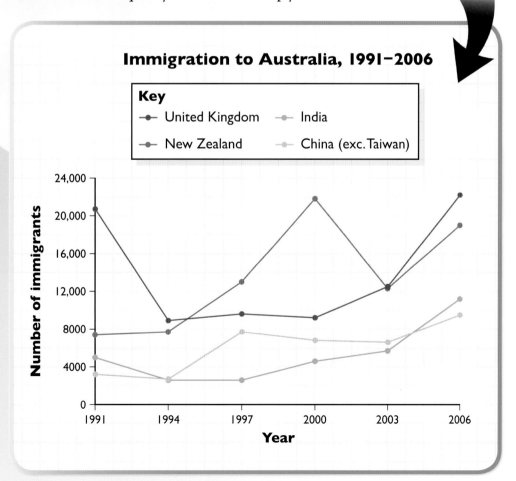

Immigration to Australia, 1991–2006

Key
- ● United Kingdom
- ● New Zealand
- ● India
- ● China (exc. Taiwan)

Refugees

Refugees are people who leave their home country because they feel they have no choice. If a country is at war, many people leave their homes and become refugees. Others may leave because they feel that the people in power in their country make it dangerous for them to stay there. Over 2.5 million people have left Iraq since the country was invaded by US troops and their **allies** in 2003. About 2 million of these refugees are in Syria and Jordan.

Natural disasters, such as earthquakes, floods, or famines can also force people to become refugees. Often, people are able to return home and rebuild their lives after a disaster. However, this is not always the case. Between 1845 and 1852, there was a terrible famine in Ireland. Over a million Irish people died, and two million more fled the country. Most of these refugees sailed across the Atlantic Ocean and settled in the US and Canada.

Other immigrants

As we saw at the start of this chapter, some people go to live in other countries as part of their jobs. **Diplomats** have to live outside their home country. People who work for charities and aid organizations live where their help is needed. Another group of immigrants are people who move abroad when they retire. People from Britain, for example, retire to warmer countries such as Spain or Italy, while many Canadians retire to Florida in the US.

Not equally welcome

Some kinds of immigrant are more welcome in their **host country** than others. More developed countries try to **recruit** people such as doctors, scientists, and businesspeople from other countries. Their skills are very valuable. The African country of Malawi, for example, has trained over 600 doctors since becoming independent in 1964. However, only 50 of these doctors actually work in Malawi. The others have moved to other countries.

Amazing fact

There are more Malawian doctors working in the city of Manchester than in the whole of Malawi itself.

Immigrant doctors

This stacked bar chart shows the percentage of immigrant doctors and the percentage of **native-born** doctors for nine countries: Australia, Canada, Finland, France, Germany, New Zealand, Portugal, the United Kingdom, and the United States. The number above each bar shows the total number of doctors in that country. In Finland, a high percentage of the doctors are immigrants, whereas in the US most doctors are native-born.

However, Finland has only 1,114 doctors in total, whereas the US has over 790,000. This means that the US has many more immigrant doctors (213,000) than Finland (1003), even though this represents a smaller percentage of the total.

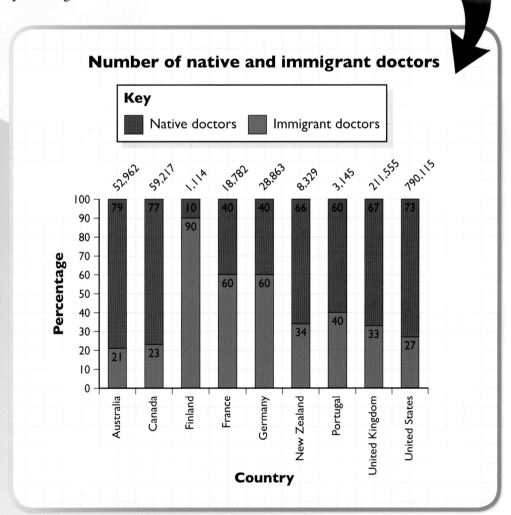

Number of native and immigrant doctors

When immigrants come to a new country, life can be difficult for them. When they first arrive, many immigrants have nowhere to live, no job, and little money. Often they can speak only a few words of the language of their new country.

High expectations

Immigrants who move because they want a better life often have high expectations of their new country. They may have seen programmes on TV or read magazines or books where everyone seems to have a nice house, a good job, and plenty of money.

"When we first arrived, we had trouble because we didn't speak English very well. We weren't accustomed to the customs and way of life in the US. I couldn't use the oven, turn on the faucet or shower, nor vacuum the floor because I hadn't encountered these things in my homeland."

Tina from Vietnam, talking about arriving in the US for the first time.

Ecuadorian immigrants harvest lettuce in Spain. Many immigrants have low-paid jobs in the food and farming industries.

When they arrive in their new country, immigrants often find that things are very different from how they expected them to be. Studies have shown that immigrants are more likely to have low-paid jobs than people who were born in the country. Many new immigrants are forced to take unpleasant jobs that native-born people don't want to do. These are things such as cleaning, fruit-picking, making clothing, and working in factories producing food.

Housing can also be a disappointment. Often immigrants have to live in crowded houses or flats, because of their low wages. If new immigrants do not know the language of their new country, this can make life even more difficult. As well as finding a home, working, and looking after their family, they have to learn a new language. This is harder for adults than it is for children.

Immigrant wages

This bar chart shows the results of a study done in the UK, which looked at how much money immigrants from different countries earned. On average, immigrants from the US had the best-paid jobs. Immigrants from Bangladesh and Poland earned the least. Although many immigrants have very low wages, the pay for immigrants who are encouraged to come to the UK because of their skills can be very high.

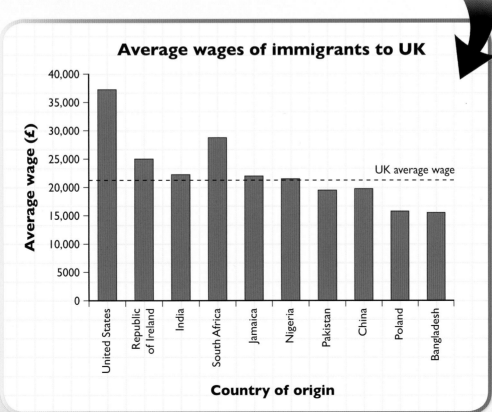

Average wages of immigrants to UK

Treated with suspicion

Immigrants are often treated with suspicion in their new country. Some native-born people believe that immigrants take jobs and houses from them. They resent the newcomers, and may insult them or even attack them.

Immigrants may also suffer from **discrimination**. This is when a person is treated badly or unfairly simply because of their skin colour or their race, or because they have a different culture or religion. In France, for example, since 2003 there has been a series of attacks on Jewish and Muslim graves and religious buildings.

 In November 2007, there was rioting near Paris, France, after two immigrants were killed in an accident with a police car. Other immigrants in the area protested because they thought the police were not taking the deaths seriously.

Broken families

Often when a family migrates to another country, they cannot afford for everyone to go at once. One member of the family makes the trip, and then brings over the rest of the family once they have saved enough money.

Reuniting families

Many of the immigrants who get permission to live in the US do so because part of their family is already living there. These pie charts show the percentage of people from four different countries who were allowed in to reunite with their family.

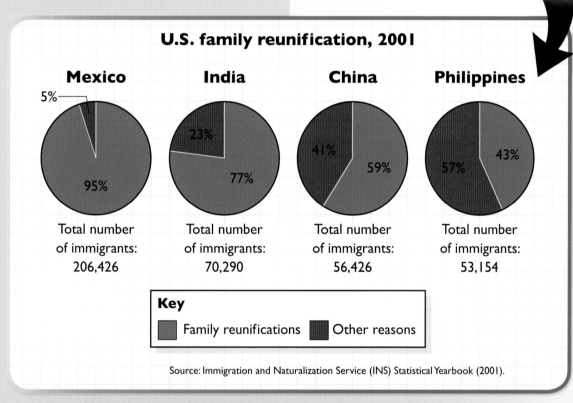

U.S. family reunification, 2001

Mexico
5%
95%

Total number of immigrants: 206,426

India
23%
77%

Total number of immigrants: 70,290

China
41%
59%

Total number of immigrants: 56,426

Philippines
57%
43%

Total number of immigrants: 53,154

Key
Family reunifications | Other reasons

Source: Immigration and Naturalization Service (INS) Statistical Yearbook (2001).

"My mom wanted to leave Mexico because she needed money to support our family. One afternoon my brother, sister, and I were in a little store which my grandma has. My mom came up to the store and said, 'I just called a taxi. I am going to the US.' Before I knew it, the taxi was there. My mom gave each of us a hug and got into the taxi and left.

"Weeks passed, and we had no news from our mom. One day, in the afternoon, I was playing outside when my grandma got a call from my mom. My grandma was relieved because my mom had made it to the States okay. Two years later my mom was able to bring us here to Virginia."

Marcelina, an immigrant to the US from Mexico.

Mixed feelings

Even when immigrants are settled and happy in their new country, they often still feel torn. Often they feel homesick for the country they have left behind, even if they were forced to leave because of war or some other disaster.

The children of immigrants grow up with a mixture of cultures. At home they learn the customs and religion of their original country, but outside the home they encounter a different culture. Sometimes they can feel torn between their homeland and their adopted country.

Mixed loyalties

Bayram is a Turkish immigrant working in Germany. He runs a bakery. Like many of the other 2 million Turks who live in Germany, he hopes one day to return to Turkey. He does not have a German passport, and most of his friends are Turkish. However, during the 2006 soccer World Cup, Bayram had a large German flag outside his bakery. He and many of his friends cheered on Germany to win.

 Natural disasters, such as floods, often force people to seek out a new country to start over in.

Building a successful life

Although life can be difficult at first, in time most immigrants do manage to settle in. Most immigrants work hard, and they are usually resourceful people (they can cope well with difficulties). This helps them to survive in their new country.

Many immigrants who find work send a large part of their wages to family back in their home country. Millions of immigrants across the world do this. Altogether, money sent home adds up to a huge sum – about $250 billion each year. In small countries such as Moldova, Tonga, and Guyana, the money sent home by immigrants adds up to more than a fifth of the country's gross national product (all the money the country earns in a year). It has a significant effect in reducing poverty.

Sending money home

Many immigrants who come to work in another country leave family members behind. If they get work and begin to earn money, they often send some of it back to their family. This bar chart shows the countries that immigrants most often send money (remittances) back to as a percentage of that country's **Gross Domestic Product** (**GDP**).

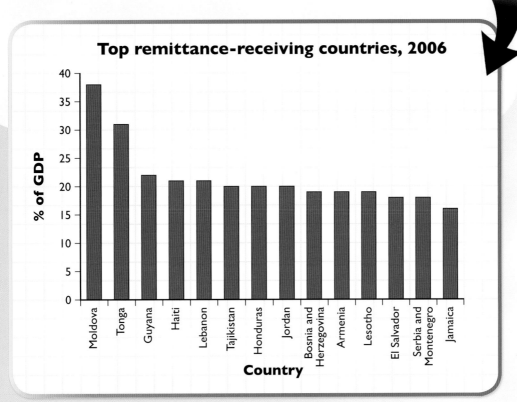

Top remittance-receiving countries, 2006

In most countries, there are laws that control who can come to live there and who cannot. These laws are different in each country. Immigrants have to apply for permission to move to another country. Immigrants must also apply for permission to work in another country. People who migrate without getting this permission are called **illegal immigrants**.

Different laws

The laws about who can move to a country and who cannot are known as a country's **immigration policy**. Some countries have a very strict immigration policy. This means that they give hardly anyone permission to move there. Japan is an example of a country that has an extremely rigid immigration policy. It is a small, crowded country, and the government is very strict about who can move there permanently.

Other countries have a more open immigration policy. They allow many people to move there to live and work. Sweden and Canada are examples of countries with this kind of immigration policy. However, most countries are between these two extremes. In general, skilled immigrants who will benefit the country are allowed to stay and work.

Less skilled immigrants are sometimes allowed to work in a country, but often only for a limited time. Many countries also take some refugees. Other countries contribute funding to aid refugees.

Citizenship tests

Immigrants who have lived in a host country for several years may want to become citizens. Many countries have a citizenship test that immigrants must pass in order to become full citizens. Can you answer this question from the UK test?

The origins of our Parliament were in the early Middle Ages. In 1215 the great barons forced King John to sign a bill of rights. What is that document called?

A: The Mappa Mundi
B: The Magna Carta
C: The Bill of Rights

Answer: B.

Changing conditions

In general, immigration numbers have risen since the 1960s. This has led most of the more developed countries to make their immigration laws tougher. Immigration law reform has always been a debated topic in the US, especially during election time. Even countries such as Spain, which until recently was encouraging many immigrants, now have stricter rules about how many immigrants they will allow in the country.

Illegal immigrants arrested

Most immigrants from Asia into Europe travel via Turkey, and from here into Greece, where many of them stay. Most of these immigrants are illegal. This bar graph shows the numbers of illegal immigrants arrested by Greek border guards each year.

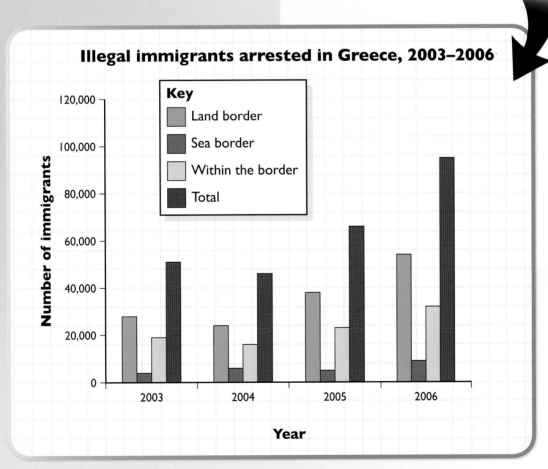

Illegal immigrants arrested in Greece, 2003–2006

Key
- Land border
- Sea border
- Within the border
- Total

Number of immigrants

Year

Why do people become illegal immigrants?

When people are not allowed to enter a country legally, they sometimes try to get there illegally instead. Many illegal immigrants are refugees who have been forced to leave their country because of war or disaster. They often escape to a neighbouring country, where they may have to live in a **refugee camp**. If that country will not let them enter as refugees, they may try to get into another country illegally.

Other illegal immigrants cross into another country because they are living in poverty. The biggest problem with illegal immigrants in the world is on the border between Mexico and the US. Poor people from Mexico try to cross illegally into the United States because they can earn more money there. Close to one million people are arrested each year trying to cross the border between the US and Mexico. Many more people cross without being caught and enter the country illegally.

 These illegal immigrants are from Africa. They were trying to cross to Italy, but were caught by Italian Coast Guards.

Arriving illegally

Immigrants crossing the border between the USA and Mexico often simply walk. In other parts of the world, people try to enter countries illegally by boat. For example, many small boats carrying illegal immigrants make the trip from north or west Africa to Spain, France, or Italy.

Illegal immigrants may also enter a country legally, with a short-term work permit or simply a holiday **visa**. They then stay in the country illegally after their permit or visa runs out. In most countries, if you are married to a citizen of that country, you have a right to live there. Because of this some immigrants pay for fake marriages, arranged over the internet, as a way of getting into a country.

Coyotes

Over 10,000 border guards patrol the border between the US and Mexico. This makes it difficult for illegal immigrants to avoid being caught. Many of them pay smugglers, or "coyotes", to help them get across the border. The coyotes know the border area very well. They charge large fees to guide illegal immigrants across without getting caught.

Illegal immigration in the US

This line graph shows the estimated numbers of illegal immigrants into the US, for every year from 1980 to 2005.

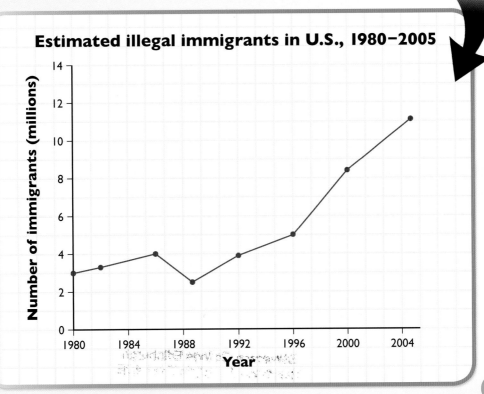

Estimated illegal immigrants in U.S., 1980–2005

Number of immigrants (millions) — Year

 A US border agent guards a group of illegal immigrants. They were caught trying to cross the border from Mexico into the US.

Dangers for illegal immigrants

Many people die each year trying to cross illegally from one country into another country. People crossing from Africa to Europe, or from south-east Asia to Australia, often make the trip in small, old, overcrowded boats. Sometimes the boats sink at sea, killing everyone on board.

A large part of the border area between Mexico and the US is very hot, dry desert. Some people walk across the desert, others cross in the back of trucks. Each year between 300 and 500 people die trying to cross the border.

Immigrants travelling from Asia to Europe are also often smuggled in large container trucks. The journey can take several days. During this time, the immigrants are trapped in the back of the truck. Sometimes the people run out of food, water, or air during the trip. In 2000, 58 Chinese immigrants died in the back of a truck travelling from Asia to the UK, when their only air vent closed up.

"When I came to the United States for the first time it was very hard for me to cross the border. I spent two weeks in Tijuana trying to cross the border. The INS [border guards] caught me and put me in jail for one month. My family thought I had died."

Remigio, who tried to cross illegally from Mexico to the US.

Theft and slavery

There are many other dangers for people travelling to a country illegally. Immigrants trying to reach a new country by boat are often stopped by armed criminal gangs in fast boats, who steal anything valuable they have with them. Many illegal immigrants rely on smugglers to help them travel from their home to a new country.

The smugglers charge large amounts of money for this. Often they force the immigrants to work for them once they arrive, in order to pay for the cost of the trip. The immigrants work long hours in terrible conditions, and receive little or no pay for it. They are treated like slaves, but they cannot complain because they are in the country illegally.

Crimes against immigrants

The two pie charts below show the different ways in which criminals exploit male and female immigrants. Most men are exploited for their labour. This means that they are sometimes made to work long hours for very low pay. Women are exploited in other ways. They are often used as slaves rather than workers.

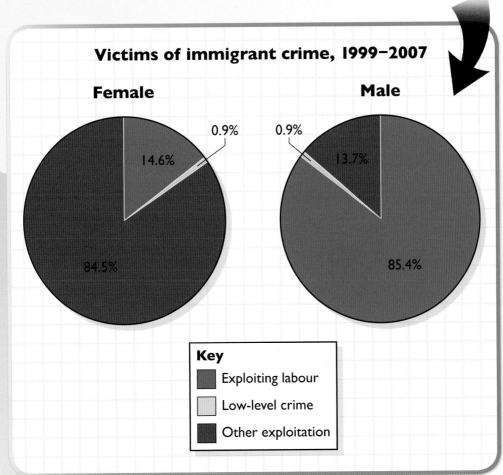

Victims of immigrant crime, 1999–2007

Female

0.9%
14.6%
84.5%

Male

0.9%
13.7%
85.4%

Key
- Exploiting labour
- Low-level crime
- Other exploitation

Costs and benefits

Some people believe that allowing immigrants into a country is a bad idea. They say that immigrants take jobs and homes that could go to local people. Immigrants work for less money, which means that local people also have to work for less in order to get work. This reduces wages overall. Also, immigrants claim many benefits and use health care that should be for local people.

However, studies do not back up these ideas. We have already seen that immigrants do many of the dirty or unpleasant jobs that others do not want to do. Often they do work for low wages, but over the whole country this has little effect. And studies have shown that immigrants actually use fewer benefits and less health care than native-born people.

 Below, immigrants to the US are taking an English class. Learning the language of the host country is necessary if people really want to settle in a new country.

Immigrant scientists are essential in developing new ideas in science.

Sometimes, when many immigrants arrive in a particular area within a short space of time, it can cause some difficulties. Schools, for example, can have trouble coping with large numbers of children who are new to the country, especially if they speak another language.

Immigrants do also bring advantages to their adopted country. Without immigrants, it would be difficult to find people to do many essential jobs. Immigrants can add to the richness of a country's culture. In the US, foods such as bagels and pizza were originally brought to the country by immigrants. Immigrant scientists and engineers helped to develop telephones, mains electricity, rockets, and other important inventions.

Nikola Tesla (1856–1943)

Nikola Tesla moved to the USA from Croatia in Eastern Europe. He built the first practical mains electricity system in 1895. Tesla worked in Hungary, then in France, before moving to the US. He arrived in New York with nothing except a letter of recommendation from his old boss to Thomas Edison. It said, "I know two great men and you are one of them; the other is this young man."

Past and future

If we look at immigration in the past, we can see that it was very different from today. In the 1800s, most immigrants to the US were Germans, rather than Mexicans. The largest wave of immigrants to the US came from southern and eastern Europe in the early 1900s. In the 1950s and 1960s many immigrants from South Asia and the Caribbean were arriving in the UK. By 2004, the immigrants were coming from Poland rather than from India or Jamaica.

If immigration patterns are always changing, how will they change in the future? The International Organization for Migration has made some predictions, based on how the world population is likely to change. By 2050, most developed countries will have nearly a quarter fewer people of working age, if there is no immigration. This is because the birth rate (the number of babies born each year) is falling in most developed countries. By this time, the number of people of working age in Africa will have risen from 400 million today to over 1 billion.

 A crowd gathers at a Miami, Florida, festival. Miami has a large immigrant population, which continues to grow.

Another change that could affect immigration in the future is climate change. Scientists predict that the overall temperature of the Earth will rise in the future because of pollution from carbon dioxide and other gases. Changes in weather patterns could lead to large migrations of people. Some places will become too hot and dry for people to live there comfortably, so they will need to move. The warmer climate will also melt ice, which will cause sea levels to rise. Low-lying areas such as the Pacific island of Nauru are already suffering regular floods because of rises in sea levels.

Coping with immigration

If future predictions are correct, then there are likely to be more and more immigrants in the future. However, this could be a good thing. It will bring more richness and variety to human societies. And if we live in communities where people from many cultures mix, we may become more tolerant of differences between people, and learn to live in harmony.

 This map is a prediction of what the world's climate might be like around 2055. The colours orange and red indicate the largest changes. Temperature rises are predicted to be larger over land than over the ocean and largest of all in the north.

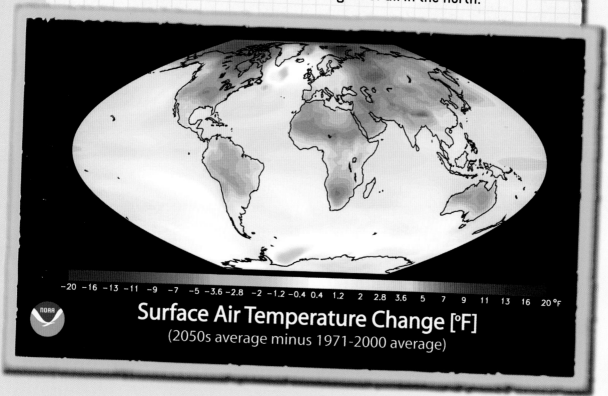

Surface Air Temperature Change [°F]
(2050s average minus 1971-2000 average)

-20 -16 -13 -11 -9 -7 -5 -3.6 -2.8 -2 -1.2 -0.4 0.4 1.2 2 2.8 3.6 5 7 9 11 13 16 20 °F

Data is information about something. We often get important data as a mass of numbers, and it is difficult to make any sense of them. Graphs and charts are ways of displaying data visually. This helps us to see relationships and patterns in the numbers. Different types of graphs or charts are good for displaying different types of information.

Bar charts

Bar charts are a good way to compare amounts of different things. Bar charts have a vertical **y-axis** showing the **scale**, and a horizontal **x-axis** showing the different types of information.

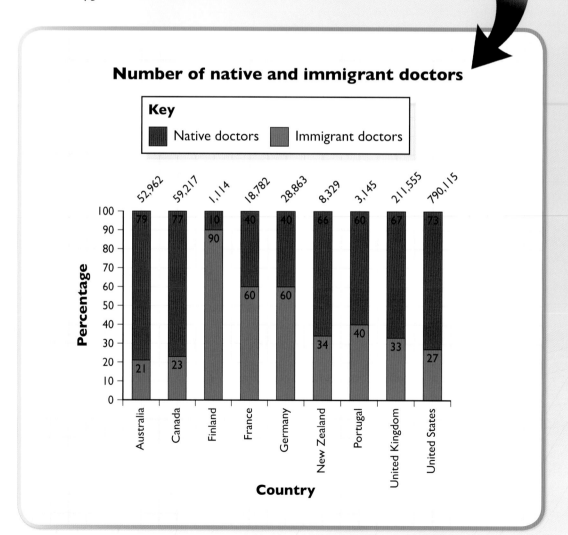

Pie charts

A pie chart is the best way to show how something is divided up. Pie charts show information as different-sized portions of a circle or slices of a "pie". They can help you compare **proportions**. You can easily see which section is the largest slice of the whole pie.

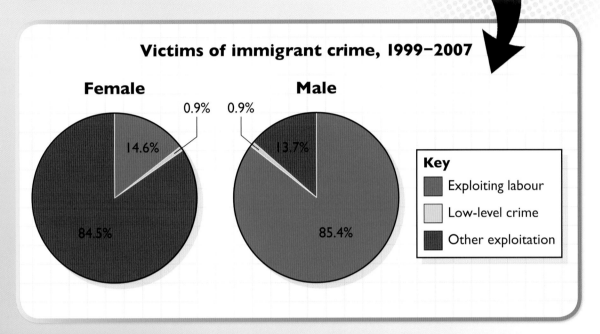

Victims of immigrant crime, 1999–2007

Female — 0.9%, 14.6%, 84.5%

Male — 0.9%, 13.7%, 85.4%

Key
- Exploiting labour
- Low-level crime
- Other exploitation

Line graphs

Line graphs use lines to join up points on a graph. They can be used to show how something changes over time. Time is usually shown on the x-axis.

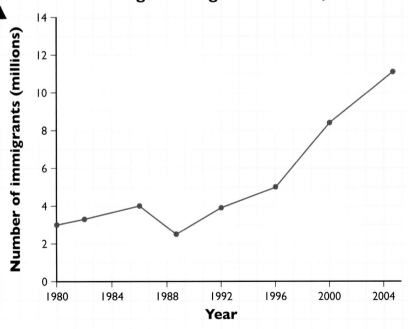

Estimated illegal immigrants in U.S., 1980–2005

Number of immigrants (millions) vs Year

GLOSSARY

allies friendly countries

ambassador person who represents the government of their home country in a foreign country

diplomat person whose job is to keep good relationships between countries

discrimination unfair treatment of a person or group of people

emigrant person who goes to live in a foreign country

emigrate go to live in a foreign country

exploit use people for personal gain

famine situation in which there is not enough food

Gross Domestic Product (GDP) total value of goods and services produced by a country

host country country that an immigrant moves to

illegal immigrant someone who moves to live in a country without getting permission to live there

immigrant person who comes to live in a foreign country

immigration policy laws about immigration in a particular country

Jamestown first English settlement in North America

migrate move country

native-born someone living in the country they were born in

population number of people that live in a country, a city, or an area

proportion size of one group of data compared to the whole set of data or to other groups

recruit encourage someone to take a job

refugee person who is forced to leave their country because of war, famine, or some similar reason

refugee camp place where a group of refugees live together in tents

scales numbered lines on a graph or chart

visa permission from the government of a country that allows an immigrant to stay in that country

x-axis horizontal axis of a graph or chart

y-axis vertical axis of a graph or chart

FURTHER INFORMATION

Books

Moving People (Geography Focus), Louise Spilsbury (Raintree, 2006)

Real Life Stories: Living as a Refugee (Ticktock Media, 2005)

Real Life Stories: Refugee Camp (Ticktock Media, 2006)

Refugee Diary: Gervelie's Journey, Anthony Robinson and Annemarie Young (Frances Lincoln Children's Books, 2008)

Why Are People Refugees? Catherine Senker (Hodder Wayland, 2004)

World Issues: Immigration, Ruth Wilson (Franklin Watts, 2004)

Websites

Find out about the history of immigration in the UK.
http://news.bbc.co.uk/hi/english/static/in_depth/uk/2002/race/short_
history_of_immigration.stm

From the United Nations Educational, Scientific and Cultural Organisation (UNESCO) homepage, click on the theme of "Social & Human Sciences," then on the theme of "Social Transformations," then on "International Migration and Multicultural Policies".
http://www.unesco.org

Read some fascinating stories of ordinary immigrants in the US.
http://www.dreamsacrossamericaonline.org/

Some examples of the questions in the UK citizenship test. How well can you do?
http://news.bbc.co.uk/1/hi/magazine/4099770.stm

INDEX